P9-EGN-671

# A New Green Day

## Antoinette Portis

NEAL PORTER BOOKS

HOLIDAY HOUSE / NEW YORK

*For Barbara Bottner, who got me started*

**Neal Porter Books**

Text and illustrations copyright © 2020 by Antoinette Portis
All Rights Reserved
HOLIDAY HOUSE is registered in the U.S. Patent and Trademark Office.
Printed and bound in December 2019 at Toppan Leefung, DongGuan City, China.
The artwork for this book was made using brush and sumi ink, leaf prints, vine charcoal and
hand-stamped lettering. Color was added digitally.
www.holidayhouse.com
First Edition
10   9   8   7   6   5   4   3   2   1

Cataloging-in-Publication Data is available from the Library of Congress

"Morning lays me on your pillow,
an invitation, square and warm.
Come out and play!"

says sunlight.

"I scribble on the walk
in glistening ink.
Read all about my
nighttime travels,"

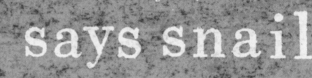

says snail.

"I'm a map of my own
green home.
Follow my roads
and climb,"

says leaf.

"When I move,
I measure.
I'll count out tickles
across your hand,"

says
inchworm.

"I'm a comma
in the long, long sentence
of the stream.
Someday soon,
you'll hear my croak,"

says tadpole.

"I'm a candy sucked smooth
in the river's mouth.
Let me sweeten your pocket,"

says pebble.

"I'm a mountain
that moves.
Look,
I come to you,"

says cloud.

"I'm a chorus
of a million tiny voices.
Come splash
in my song,"

says rain.

"I slash the sky
with my bright fangs.
Warning! Run inside!
I can bite a tree in two!"

says    lightning.

"I'm the rumble
in the stomach of the storm.
(Pardon me—
must be something I ate),"

MUMBLE
GRUMBLE
BOOM

says thunder.

"I am cool pudding
on a muggy day.
Let your toes
have a taste!"

says mud.

"I race up the hill
while lying at your feet.
Wave at me
and I'll wave at you,"

says shadow.

"I'm a black coat
slipped around
Earth's shoulders.
Count my shiny buttons,"

says night.

"I am the engine
of the summer dark.
Sleep, while I thrum
in your tomorrow,"

says cricket.

"And a new green day."